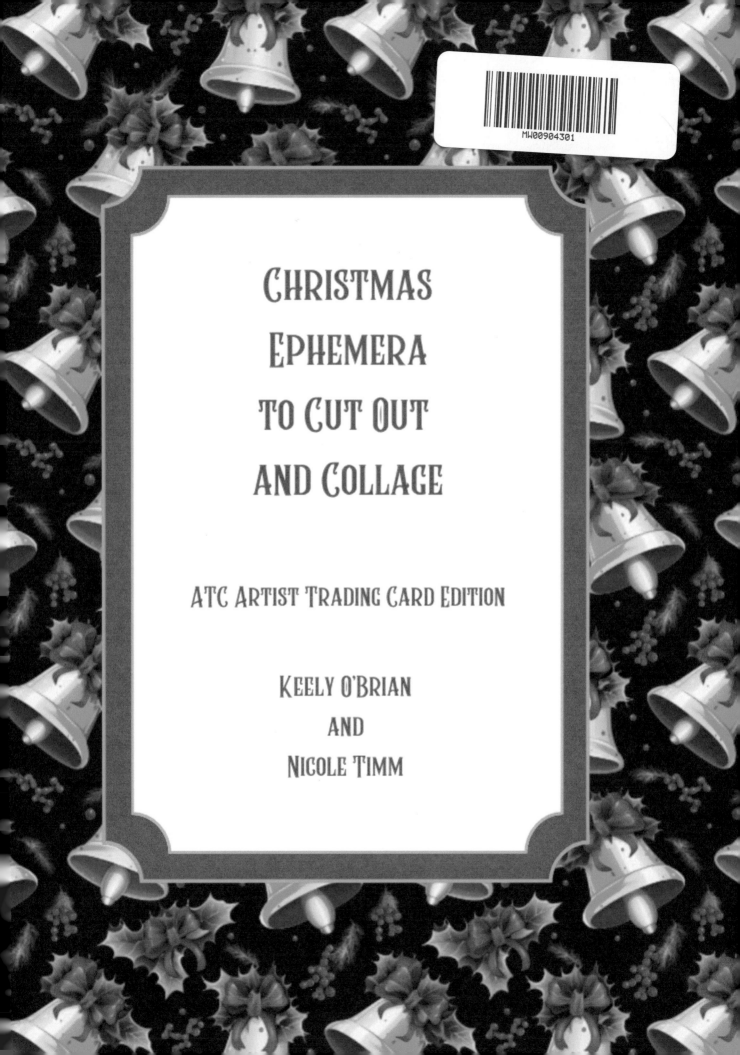

Christmas Ephemera to Cut Out and Collage

ATC Artist Trading Card Edition

Keely O'Brian
and
Nicole Timm

Dear Friends,

We're so excited to share our first collaboration,
**Christmas Ephemera To Cut Out and Collage - ATC
Artist Trading Cards Edition!**
It's packed with cute Christmas things to cut and collage.
There are also background papers for you to have fun
and play with too. The images are also great for
postcards, Christmas cards, journals, glue books & more.
Here are some of Nicole's cute and adorable ATCs for
inspiration.

Happy Crafting!

Love Keely & Nicole

Relax.
Cut.
Glue.

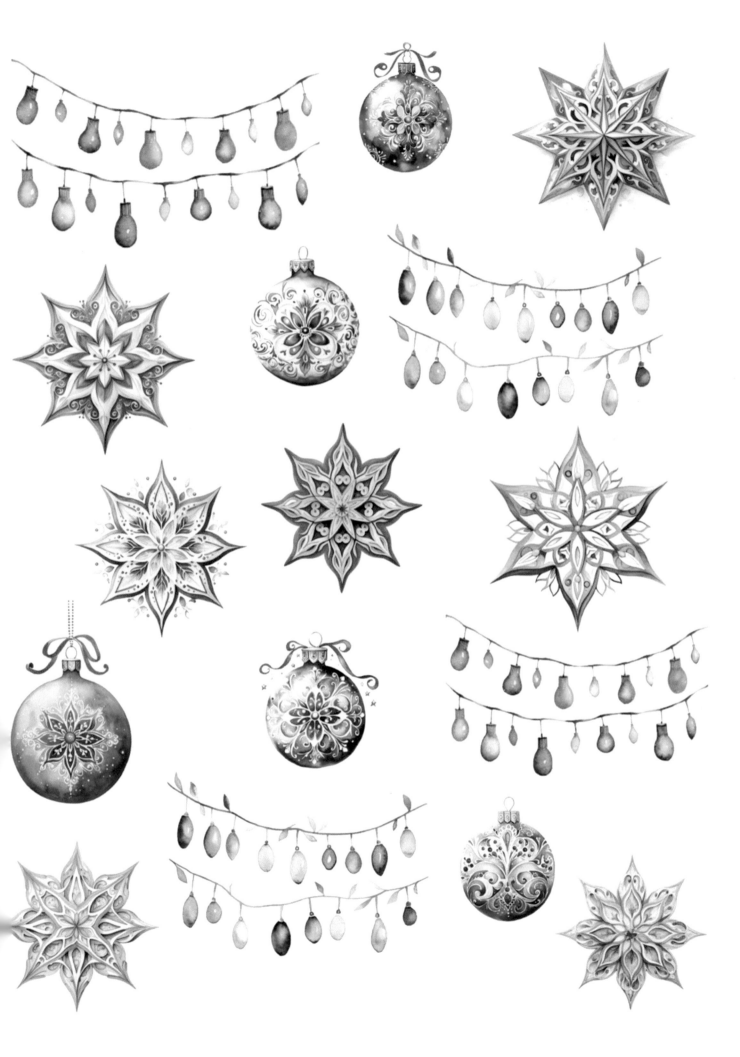

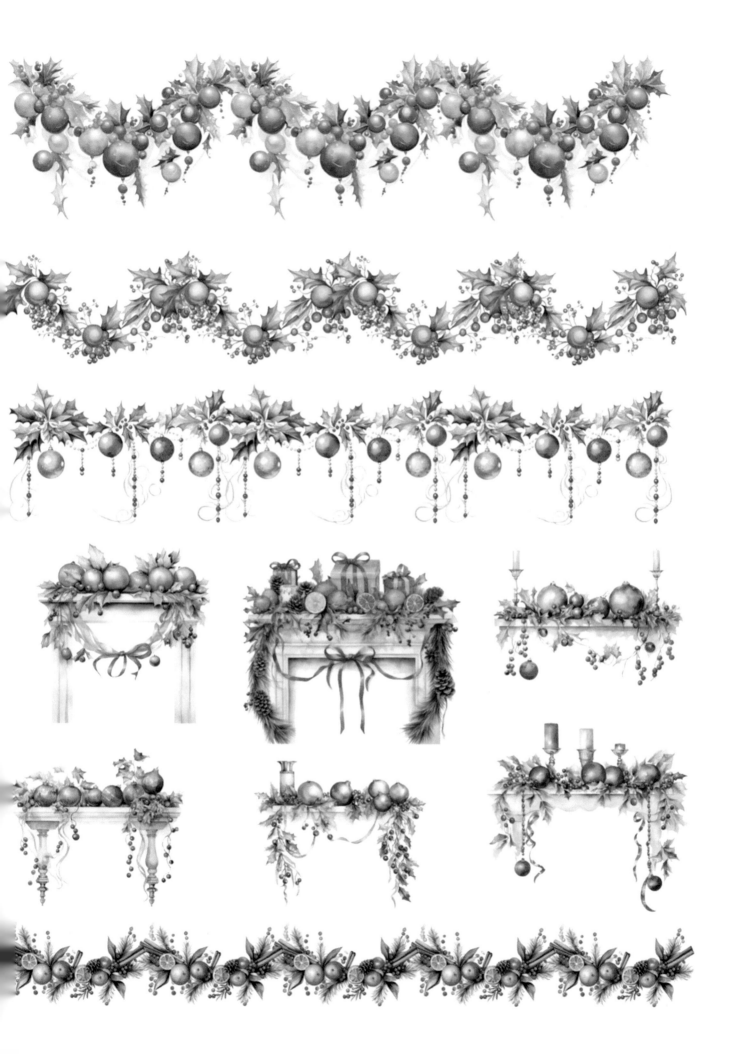

Merry Christmas

Let it snow	Joy	Deck The Halls
Jingle Bells	Happy Holidays	Merry and Bright
Santa's Helpers	Cheer	Christmas Wishes
Season's Greetings	Santa	Holly Jolly
Believe	December	Eggnog Time!
Winter Wonderland	Ho Ho Ho	Frosty The Snowman
Peace	Mistletoe	Holly Berries
Merry & Bright	Gingerbread	Christmas Wreath
T'is the season	Jolly	Crackers
Fa La La	Rejoice	Ding Dong Merrily!
Comfort and Joy	Holly	Christmas Bells
Christmas Cheer		Sleigh Bells Ring

Made in United States
Troutdale, OR
12/05/2024

25931899R00048